ISLAND

FABER ƒƒ MUSIC

London, *c.* 2003
Photo: Alex Lake

CONTENTS

Sketches throughout: Tom Chaplin

FOREWORD

When you first get into music, quite often it's all about the energy – maybe the melodies and rhythm too. We definitely felt that way. But the first band Richard and I really got into were Pet Shop Boys, and journalists always made specific reference to Neil Tennant's lyrics (normally describing them as sardonic or tongue-in-cheek, but to us they seemed powerfully heartfelt) and I started to pay more attention to what their songs were saying about people, society, the world. Radio 1 had a competition where listeners had to decipher the lyrics of R.E.M.'s 'The Sidewinder Sleeps Tonite'. U2 grabbed phrases from films and the art world for their *Achtung Baby* album and flashed up lyrics and topical buzzwords on their *Zoo TV* tour. Words, ideas, stories became a much bigger part of our musical life. We became obsessed with Radiohead's mournful, thrilling *OK Computer* and tried to learn from Thom Yorke's blending of grand emotional landscapes with hyper-mundane details. Paul Simon's poetic, painstakingly crafted solo work gave us something to aspire to and Nick Drake's aching verse taught us the beauty of a more delicate touch. Most of all, The Smiths' amazing knack for pairing deeply emotional lyrics with wildly catchy melodies made a huge impression.

Inevitably we wrote a lot of bad and mediocre songs over many years. We were playing in pubs around London trying to capture, and hold, people's attention – and on stage we learned what our strengths were (and weren't). Looking back, I think that, like so many bands of that era, we had been trying to channel Radiohead's edgy energy or Oasis' psychedelic swagger to frame whatever we had to say about ourselves and the world we saw around us; and there came a point where we realised that tone didn't come naturally to us. It felt a little forced. What did come naturally was a more openly emotional approach against a background of everyday life in small towns; little snapshots of life that, like the music of The Smiths or Nick Drake, held their emotional power within apparently quite mundane settings. We felt that all of life's drama was contained within even the most 'normal' lives and the most apparently unassuming streets and people. We seemed to be better at writing about moments of our own lives in a true and not very glamorous way – and, maybe because the lyrics were flecked with details that rang true, the songs started to connect with people.

Around 2001 we hit a seam of writing that felt 'right' and some good songs started to fall into place. The first one I remember feeling was a step up for us, and also had a distinctive style of our own, was 'To the End of the Earth'. It contained a lot of themes and images that we've returned to extensively over the years.

Like a lot of our songs at that time, I wrote that with my little Yamaha PSR-48 keyboard on my knees, sitting in the flat I shared with Tom and our guitarist Dominic in Stamford Hill. 'She Has No Time' was an early one too, followed by 'Bedshaped' and 'This is the Last Time'. Not long after that, Dominic left the band and the actual sound of our music morphed into something that matched the emotional tone of the lyrics. It took at least a couple of years before anyone else agreed, but we felt we were starting to create something really good.

Hopes and Fears is undoubtedly a very emotional album. But for the most part it's not really a romantic album. Writers and filmmakers talk about 'world-building', and similarly the most potent albums usually have a 'world' that they invent or at least occupy. They set a particular scene – you can picture the streets, the characters, the light, the colours, the weather… maybe even transporting you to a certain state of mind or way of looking at the world or at your own life. We weren't savvy enough to think about any of that when we made *Hopes and Fears*, but luckily, we found our 'world' by instinct – we just put to music episodes from our own lives, set in the streets we grew up on and the places where we spent so much time together. And really the overarching feel of the record is a sense of pushing forward, persevering, not wanting to give up – in its most literal form it's the story of the three of us trying to stick together, to stop waiting and start living, to break out of the lives we knew so well and to step into a bigger adventure. I'm not sure we saw it at the time, but listening now it's clear to me that the overarching theme of the record is actually friendship.

Tim Rice-Oxley
July 2024

San Francisco, October 2004

Photo: Jake Chessum

A dressing room somewhere, *c.* 2004
Photo: Alex Lake

BEGINNINGS

I'm sure if you asked each of us about the start of Keane you'd get three different answers, but I'm told that I met Tim as a toddler, which would have been not long before Tom was born. The first time I remember spending time with him was when I was about 11, when we found ourselves in the same class at school. This would have been around 1986. We quickly became really good friends, bonding over a shared love of music (especially the Pet Shop Boys) and sports of pretty much any kind. We lived at opposite ends of Battle, a small town in Sussex, close enough to spend lots of the school holidays together. Around that time I got to know Tim's younger brother Tom, and Tom's best friend, who was also called Tom (Chaplin)... I would ride my bike to Tim's house and we spent endless days playing football and cricket in the garden, the four of us making for some pretty competitive two against two games, often ending with the last tennis ball lost on the roof of their house, or the rain falling... at which point we would retreat inside and watch TV or a video... I particularly remember Queen – Live at Wembley (from 1986) and Simon and Garfunkel's Concert in Central Park (1981). I remember us having a bunch of the *Now That's What I Call Music...* chart

hit compilations on double cassette; Tears for Fears – *Songs from the Big Chair*; Tracy Chapman; and everything the Pet Shop Boys had released.

I took the photo of Tim and Tom by some fallen trees at school in about 1988.

When we moved schools in 1989, Tim and I both went to the same one and were still in a lot of the same classes. I think by that point we had got into Paul Simon's *Graceland* and *ChangesBowie* and were starting to get exposed to more and more music from the older kids at school. Ride were popular, along with Carter USM, and for some reason the soundtrack to *The Lost Boys*. We were really into INXS too, and had started to read Q magazine, the *NME* and *Melody Maker*. Tim was getting pretty good at the piano by this point, so by our early teens we were playing through a lot of different music, including various songs from the 'It's easy to play…' series of books. I remember… The Beatles; Paul Simon; and Roy Orbison editions got a lot of use. These books laid out song chords and words together, and were a brilliant way to learn. I guess by then Tim's brain had started to think in terms of songwriting and song structure, and we both started to learn how to sing harmonies.

Among our new friends was a very good piano and violin player, Dominic Scott. Dom's family was from Dublin, and in 1991 he discovered the album *Achtung Baby*, and got a red Squier Stratocaster (cheap Fender guitar copy) and an amplifier. In seemingly no time he had worked out how to play it really well – the guitar just seemed to come naturally to him.

Around this time, perhaps inspired by Dom's ability to play lots of the songs on *Achtung Baby*, which was a record we all loved, I finally decided to ask my parents if I could take drum lessons. Despite me being at a posh private school, my family was not particularly wealthy and I was there on a scholarship. Musical instrument lessons were extra, and pretty expensive, but I had wanted to try drums for a long time and my parents generously agreed, so around 1991 I started lessons… in the drum shed, which the school had wisely positioned out on its own in the middle of nowhere. I loved listening to the drums, especially Larry Mullen Jnr., Bill Berry and Ringo. My playing drums gave Tim an idea… how about we get Dom on guitar, with Tim and his trusty Yamaha PSR-48 keyboard – we could play music together in the drum shed! I cannot imagine how bad we sounded, but I do remember how much fun it was. There must have been a microphone and some kind of speakers too. I remember being incredibly pleased when a friend said he had heard us playing 'One' by U2 – I couldn't believe he could even recognise the song. Vocals were handled by Tim or Dom, both good singers. I don't think we had a name, but we had begun, and would learn as we went. Dom had some kind of effects pedal (Boss or Zoom) and was soon experimenting with delay, chorus, reverb, overdrive, and combinations of them, making brilliant guitar sounds inspired by The Edge. Playing together gave us all something new to do in the school holidays, but Dom had to go back to Ireland so he would either have to travel over to stay with one of us, or we would get the train and ferry to Dublin. Tim and Dom were writing songs and we were listening to more and more music in what was a golden age for young British bands. I loved *Violator* by Depeche Mode and A-Ha, and Tim was getting into The Smiths.

We were a band before we knew it. I am trying to recall when Tom joined, but I honestly can't remember. I guess it was the mid-90s – I think Tim suggested it. Tom was a brilliant singer, and was already playing music with a friend of his. He was also quite a lot younger than Tim and me, and varying degrees of hilarious, loud and occasionally very annoyingly mischievous (even before we gave him a microphone and invited him to be the focus of attention!). He particularly loved charismatic singers like Freddie Mercury and Michael Jackson, and was starting to write good songs. Tim and I had got pretty deep into The Beatles, had been blown away by U2's multimedia extravaganza Zoo TV tour at Wembley (1993), and seen my beloved R.E.M.'s Monster tour at Milton Keynes in 1995 – that line-up was unbelievable: Sleeper (who I loved); Radiohead (*The Bends* had just come out); The Cranberries at their absolute height of brilliance; and finally the wonderful R.E.M. They were incredible. Michael Stipe was captivating, the sound was huge, and I got to watch Bill play drums for the first time. It was magical. I still have a tape I recorded off the radio of the other night they played there, which was broadcast live on Radio 1. I remember Tim and I got the first train back home the following morning to get back to our summer jobs, exhausted but on a wave of adrenaline from the night before.

By this point we had left school but were still trying to be a guitar band, with Tim on bass, Tom acoustic guitar and vocals, and Dom lead electric guitar. Dom came over to write and rehearse in holidays during his time at Trinity College, Dublin. Tim and I went to (the same) university in London, and so were able to hang out a lot. Tim made friends with a guy called Adam, who would become (and still is) our manager, and another guy called Chris, who was putting a band together, initially called Starfish, but later to become Coldplay.

By the time Tom left school in 1997 we had a fair few original songs together, the writing pretty equally split between Tim, Tom and Dom, plus some half-decent covers of a few songs, including 'Paperback Writer' and 'Don't Look Back in Anger'. We recorded a few demos on a 4-track cassette recorder that Tim and I bought second-hand from someone in Brighton. Tom had a gap year job at a school in South Africa, and I remember sending him off with a copy of the recently released *OK Computer* by Radiohead. It blew all our minds. On his return, we ambushed Tom with the news that we had booked our first gig for 13th July 1998, at the Hope and Anchor in Islington, North London.

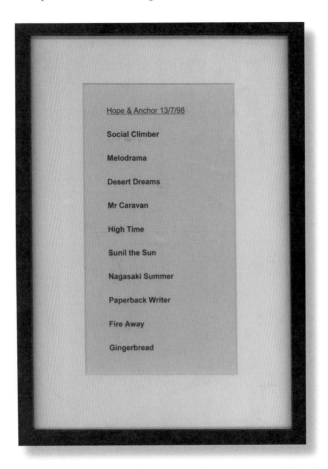

Hope & Anchor 13/7/98

Social Climber

Melodrama

Desert Dreams

Mr Caravan

High Time

Sunil the Sun

Nagasaki Summer

Paperback Writer

Fire Away

Gingerbread

We had about two weeks to get ready, and were driven up in an old Ford Transit van by Tom's older brother Jim, being stopped by the police on the way, who thought we had stolen all the instruments… like we weren't nervous enough already. I can't remember if we were before or after another band, Eric Red, but I do remember the sound engineer saying Tom's vocals were the loudest they had ever heard, and there being a few people there for the show – Tim's friends Chris (Martin) and Jonny (Buckland) were in the audience, along with our girlfriends; Adam; and anyone else we could persuade to watch us. Probably 20 or so people if you include Eric Red. Tim may have started our first ever live show with the wrong note… I couldn't possibly have noticed as I was so nervous. I think the adrenaline meant we rushed through 30 minutes of songs in about 25 minutes, but we had done it and it felt brilliant.

Tim, Dom and I were coming to the end of university, but Tom was just starting, and in faraway Scotland. We kept on writing and rehearsing whenever we could, but it was becoming pretty clear that we needed to up our commitment. We managed to persuade Tom to quit university, and we all got jobs and moved to Stamford Hill (Tim, Tom and Dom) and Newington Green (me) so we could rehearse weekly and play more gigs. There was a brilliant circuit of smallish venues in London back then – the Bull and Gate in Kentish Town; Camden had the Monarch / Dublin Castle / Falcon and many more, and we set about playing as many of those as we could, firstly as Cherry Keane, then just Keane. Adam took pity on us and started to help get us organised, taking photos of us, making demo tapes to send to venues and helping us get better gig bookings, and even organising his own shows for us to play. We were improving our home recordings, allowing us to give or sell some tapes and CDs to friends, and we then borrowed an 8-track recorder to give us more options, and then eventually recorded in the cheapest studios we could find. Tom was getting really into the engineering side of recording, and all three songwriters were writing better and better songs. Gigs were improving, and thanks to Adam and the support of friends and families we were getting larger audiences along (the venues just wanted to sell drinks, so bigger crowds meant the offer of better slots, like Friday or Saturday nights).

Guttridge's Yard, July 1998
Photo: Adam Tudhope

Somehow Adam had got the attention of a producer called Mark Wallis, who agreed to make a demo of our song 'Wolf at the Door' in a proper studio – Soho Recording Studios on Torrington Place in Soho. He had a computer whizz called James Sanger working with him, who had just worked on Dido's mega smash hit debut album. We were there all night – I remember leaving with Tim and walking through Soho as the sun was coming up. I think at these times you convince yourself that any kind of opportunity like this would be the start of big things. It wasn't. We handmade 50 copies of a beautiful CD, but it went nowhere. James Sanger stayed in touch though, and said he was building a studio in an amazing farmhouse he had bought in Normandy. He invited us to come over and record more music. This did not go as we had planned…

FRANCE, JULY 2001

We were all set to go to France when Dominic decided to quit and go back to Ireland. This was not in the plan. Tim and Tom had to give up their flat in Stamford Hill and move back to Sussex. I couldn't pay rent but my sister very kindly let me and my girlfriend live in her flat in Clapham while she was away… just another in the long list of kindnesses and generous acts that we were so lucky to have along the way. The three of us packed everything up into our cars and headed for France. Portsmouth to Cherbourg ferry, then about an hour's drive south. James's farmhouse studio was definitely spectacular but definitely wasn't a recording studio and was barely a house. It was a slow start – he seemed more interested in showing us the guns he was allowed to own in France than setting up for recording. Eventually he told me to set my drums up in a hay barn, and the other instruments went in the only room with a good floor, lights and power. The sleeping arrangements weren't much better – Tim and Tom shared a sprawling, drafty, dusty room with a hole in the floor. Elsewhere there was a functioning kitchen and bathroom, and a single bedroom for me, with a squeaky wooden bed that must have been a century old at least. James already had an engineer there, Nathan, who seemed to have been tasked with going through an endless pile of vinyl, sampling any loop or interesting part that he could find. I can't remember where he slept. There was heating in part of the house, but not the part where Tim and Tom were staying – they had to burn old floorboards and any other bits of dry wood to heat their room. There was no TV (this was pre-internet), and the only entertainment we had was *Spaced* Series 1 on DVD, a quirky British comedy by Simon Pegg and Jessica Hynes (née Stevenson) – we got to know it word for word, scene by scene.

The room with power and the new floor became the studio, but it wasn't in any way treated or organised for recording drums, amplifiers and so on, so we basically had to reinvent ourselves for the time being at least… minus the guitar, but with access to James's incredible keyboards (including a Perspex-cased Gleeman – absolutely priceless these days), and James's drum programming. We worked on a few songs that would make it onto *Hopes and Fears*, but because we had no money to pay for his time and 'studio', we offered James a cut of any future royalties, which is why he is credited on a few songs. I don't remember a huge amount of the day-to-day process, but I do recall Tim and I recording the solo on 'She Has No Time' long into one night – it was on a very tricky keyboard, and had to be played absolutely perfectly or the sound would start to change and the take had to be scrapped. I think Tim finally got it right on take 63 or 64 – a heroic effort. Tim was writing more and more songs – the walnut tree that is referenced in one was in the courtyard of this farmhouse, and I think 'Sunshine' was written underneath it. A few songs started to take shape, but time was passing, it was getting cold, and we really didn't have much money for food or to go back home and see our loved ones. I remember going to the beach nearby to get a mobile signal from across the water in Jersey, which meant not paying for international calls, and eating as much as we could from the gardens – James had employed someone to plant fruit and vegetables, although they had left with it half-done. Nevertheless there were some spuds to be dug up, which saved us a bit of money.

At one point someone went back to England, returning with a DVD of… *Spaced* Series 2! It was one of the greatest moments of the trip, but as we moved towards the autumn the mood was beginning to sour. There was no progress with building any real studio. We were running out of money and James was running out of patience. We knew we had to leave, but needed to take the recordings… the only way to get them from the computer was to secretly make a copy, which would take many hours. Nathan helped us hatch a plan. One Saturday or Sunday morning James had a shooting competition about an hour away, which would give us a window of a few hours to make the backup. It was like one of those scenes in *Mission Impossible* when you are glued to the 'making a copy' progress bar as time passes… and, sure enough, James got back before it had finished. I was dispatched to intercept him on the way to the studio. All I could think of was to feign interest in every detail of his shooting competition, and suggest I get him a drink and we sit and he could tell me all about it, until I finally got the thumbs-up from the studio. Shortly afterwards we booked a ferry home and left early one morning, hoping not to wake James. I am not sure I have seen him since.

Armed with these recordings, and a new non-guitar sound, we took over a room in Tim's parents' house in Battle to start working out how to play gigs as a three-piece. Tim was much better suited to playing piano than bass, and Tom felt freed-up by not having to play the acoustic. We needed to put some music on a computer, which we would then play along with. We needed a laptop to run this, and I had to play in time with it. Tim remembered a book called Making Music by George Martin which mentioned a clever Yamaha CP-70 stage piano that supposedly sounded great (and looked awesome) so we tracked one down and bought it – discovering that it fitted in our ageing little Ford Fiestas when taken apart.

Armed with this makeshift setup, which included a folding picnic table and some offcuts of foam to stop the laptop shaking, we struck out to play our first shows as a three-piece. When we heard the piano through the PA at the first show I think we knew we might just get away with it. The CP-70 sounds massive, and with a bit of backup from the laptop we made a pretty decent noise at our first proper live show as a three, at the Night and Day in Manchester, in front of a wonderful music publishing A&R person called Caroline Elleray and, if I am not mistaken, Mark Radcliffe from Radio 1. Caroline was soon to change our lives. She worked at BMG Music Publishing, and with her colleague Ian Ramage decided to sign us. Publishers own the songs, and Caroline and Ian believed in ours. Along with a publishing contract came an advance (actual money!) and finally a tiny bit of breathing space. Caroline brought along a huge amount of credibility and was able to put our demos in front of important people who would take notice – she had not that long before signed Coldplay (and she continues to find and nurture talent to this day at Second Songs). Simon Williams from the now-legendary Fierce Panda Records came to see us play at the Betsey Trotwood pub in Clerkenwell, London, on 19 December 2002. Fierce Panda had released first singles from, among others, The Bluetones, Supergrass, Ash, Death Cab for Cutie, Coldplay, Placebo… and soon after offered to release 500 copies of a single for us – all we had to do was send music and artwork. That single was 'Everybody's Changing', mixed by Nathan Thomas – the guy who we first met doing the sampling at James Sanger's place in France. Steve Lamacq had been to see a gig, and played 'Everybody's Changing' on his radio show… this was a huge break, and got us more attention.

It all started to become a bit of a whirlwind at that point. We did our first tour – just the three of us in a van, Tim and I driving and Tom in the back on a load of old cushions on top of the equipment. Adam arranged a trip to America to play the Mercury Lounge in New York and The Viper Room in LA. I remember waking up in our shared hotel room in NY, us all walking to a diner (I had coffee and pancakes like in the movies) and seeing Radio City Music Hall. I don't remember much about LA, except a late-night car trip to find the HOLLYWOOD sign, and a lot of trips to offices and fancy houses in Beverly Hills where execs from various record companies tried to persuade us to sign with them. It was absolutely nuts.

We went on to release another single with Fierce Panda, 'This is the Last Time', but we knew by then we would be signing with a bigger label, and at long last it looked like we might get to make an album…

Richard Hughes
July 2024

Reading Festival, August 2003
Photo: Tim Rice-Oxley

keane
LIVE 2003

Everybody's Changing
The debut single out now on Fierce Panda Records

"Everybody's Changing is an indisputably mighty pop song"
New Musical Express (NME)

"They're no ordinary trio. It's a drummer, keyboard player and a singer who has an enormous, likeable voice ...big, bold, soaring songs."
Steve Lamacq - Radio 1

FRIDAY 15th
EDINBURGH
UNDERBELLY

KEANE

Barfly Club @ The Falcon   15/01/2000
234 Royal College St. NW1   8.00pm

---

club WITH NO NAME
EST 1999

FRIDAY 8th SEPTEMBER
FOUR STAR MARY / SURIKI / TOBY SLATER
Featured in the hit TV show BUFFY THE VAMPIRE SLAYER as the ficticious band Dingos Ate My Baby, **Four Star Mary** are in the UK to promote their new single 'Marlene'. Support for the tour are fellow Americans **Suriki** and in Peterborough we also have **Toby Slater**.

SATURDAY 9th SEPTEMBER
HEAD-ON with KEANE
The popular HEAD-ON nights continue, as usual our d.j.s will be treating us to a real diverse mix of alternative classics old and new. This time our guest band will be London's **Keane** who have been getting lots of record company interest lately, in fact they had to cancel last months as Virgin had put them in the studio to do some demo's, catch them now.

THURSDAY 14th SEPTEMBER
YOURS / EMERY
Following the split of The Audience singer Sophie took the easy route and took Spiller to number one with 'groovejet'. But songwriter Billy carried on with the guitar music, found a new girl

---

Student Night featuring...

KEENE
@ THE WHITE HORSE MUSIC VENUE
Thurs. 23/11/00 . £3

HEAD-ON mix then... all the usual alternative hits (and misses) played by our regular and the odd guest d.j.s

THURSDAY 28th SEPTEMBER
TENNER / AUNT SPIKER
"fresh faced indie boys who can't stand still, with an average age of 21, they should be watched" Melody Maker "they sound as if they should smell of bike oil and aftershave, but not in a bad way" NME. **Tenner** are from Bath and already have released two acclaimed singles on Fierce Panda. Support from new Peterborough band **Aunt Spiker** featuring ex members of Arconna and Buzzcut.

Upstairs at THE PARK
30-32 Park Road, Peterborough
doors open 8pm.
support this club, let us know what you want, join and join in!

email: club.with.no.name@freezone.co.uk
coming soon - Tailgunner, King Adora, Foil, The Pecadiloes, Spearmint and Penthouse.....

MHP Guttridge's Yard
Moral Horse Productions
presents...
Stoke Newington Church Street

o k a z i y a

Evenings of Music and Drama

Saturday 25 July   8.00 - 9.30pm
Cherry Keane   Forget dessert beware your evening with their acoustic pop-rock
Coldplay
Lewd   Too cool to dance, Sit back and listen.
                              Sedges and bass. Swing with the funk

Sunday 26 July   8.00 - 9.30pm
Cherry Keane
Coldplay

Tuesday 28 July   8.00 - 9.30pm
Shola and Ellen   Solos and duets with piano accompaniment.
                              From Handel to Gershwin and all the highlights in between.

Wednesday 29 July   8.00 - 9.30pm
Elektra's Brother   Formerly at the Bloomsbury Theatre, MHP Theatre Company
                              presents it's acclaimed re-working of Euripides' Orestes.

Thursday 30 July   8.00 - 9.30pm

TOM
HAT   CMWYL
        POT OF GOLD
IS   THE LAST TIME
IS-NG   END OF THE EA
        WOLF
NC   SHE HAS NO
ME
        CLOSER

SPITZ/MON 3NT
2000

15th August 03   Edinburgh
w/ SKIN   Underbelly

Somewhere only we know
Bend & Break
Everybody's Changing
She Has No time
This is the last time
Can't stop now
Bedshaped.

London, c. 2003
Photo: Paul Rodwell

A dressing room somewhere, c. 2004
Photo: Alex Lake

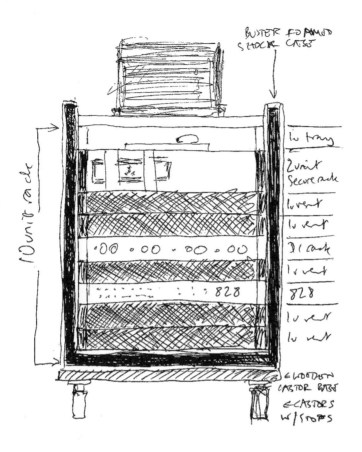

BUSTER FOAMED
SHOCK CASE

1u tray

2 unit
Secure rack

1u vent

1u vent

J1 cock

1u vent

828

1u vent

1u vent

10 unit rack

WOODEN
CASTOR BASE

CASTORS
W/ STOPS

PIANOS
Yamaha B20 9
$2500 =
$500 + 12 × $167

_____

Yamaha American Walnut
$3000 =
$600 + 12 × $200

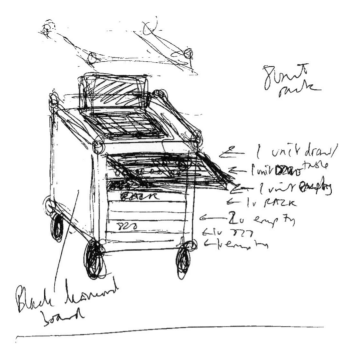

print
side

← 1 unit draw/
← 1 unit demo table
← 1 unit display
← 1v RACK
← 2v empty
← 1v 827
← ternotn

BACK

820

Black mount
board

FROM
ABOVE

Salone Strings Ensemble

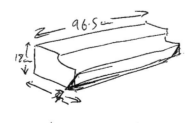

96.5

18

£115 + VAT

NOTES FROM A FRONTMAN

I have been singing for as long as I can remember. Somewhere in an old box of cassette tapes is a recording of me from when I was four years old. Armed with a Casio keyboard and a Tesco own-brand ghetto blaster, it's basically 90 minutes of me making up and singing daft songs, with my mum in the background making lunch and occasionally telling me to 'stop showing off'. In so many ways, not much has really changed – the creative streak and the desire to be heard remain undimmed, even if it's now channelled in a slightly more professional way!

Despite my passion for pop music, I think my mum and dad saw a more conventional path for harnessing my musical talents. As soon as I was at school, I joined the choir. Also, in a decision I still regret to this day, out of all the musical instrument lessons on offer, I ended up with the flute. Mind you, in those days, the idea of learning guitar or piano with an eye on how it could shape a future in a rock band was the stuff of fantasy – so perhaps the flute was no less useful a place to start than anywhere else. My first singing performance was as the Bi-Coloured-Python-Rock-Snake in a Year 1 play of Kipling's *The Elephant's Child*. All I can remember is being wedged into a two-tone sleeping bag on top of a rock and hissing a lot between lines of singing.

My first performance with the flute is one that I often think about – probably a couple of years later and in front of all the parents, I totally bottled it. Stood there in abject fear, I couldn't even get a note to come out and walked away with my head hung in shame. I remember feeling like my whole world had caved in, as though I'd be the laughing stock of the school. Once I realised that this wasn't the case, I think it probably taught me a valuable lesson about failure – it's an essential part of what spurs you on to make you better.

Being a kid in the 1980s was a pretty amazing time to fall in love with pop music. Michael Jackson and Queen (and the *Now That's What I Call Music!* compilations) were the first things that I got into. Those early influences are still key ingredients in my vocal performance today. I loved Freddie Mercury's ability to combine drama and emotion. As the school years went by, I began to gravitate more towards indie music – one of the teaching assistants gave me an album from his school days of some covers they had assembled in a half-decent recording studio – it really gave me the idea that being in a band wasn't totally out of reach. By the time I was at secondary school, Britpop was in full swing – a pretty glorious period of music and more than enough inspiration for kids wanting to form bands. This is when I think the story of Keane started to emerge…

I'd known Tim and Richard since I was a kid. Tim's younger brother (also called Tom) and I were best friends. Tim had always been the cool older brother who could bash out a tune on the piano and seemed obsessively fascinated by bits of pop music paraphernalia – sequencers, keyboards and a library of songbooks (The Beatles, Simon & Garfunkel, U2, Oasis, Blur to name but a few). Even though I'd done the odd thing with Tim over the years – mostly little performances of covers for Cherry Keen (she of Keane band name fame), we'd never really considered the idea of forming a band. I found secondary school life pretty tough. There was a lot of bullying and general teenage misery, all amplified in the pressure cooker of an old-fashioned all boys' private school. The greatest gift I received during that time was Tim teaching me how to play chords on the piano. Suddenly I had a safe and beautiful world in which I could express myself. Soon I was singing, playing and writing music that spoke to me of something bigger than the confines of that stuffy institution. Tim, Richard and their friend Dominic were already underway with an early incarnation of the band. I think I gradually became more aware (and envious) of what they had started and, as the years passed, I think they became more aware of my aspirations as a singer and songwriter. I don't think any of us are totally sure of when I first joined in with them, but I reckon it was probably in 1995 or 1996… and more than likely during a summer holiday.

The early years of Keane were fairly loose, directionless and largely about having fun; mostly convening during holidays with me, Tim and Dom contributing and singing our respective songs. My emergence as the frontman happened during that time. I would say this was largely down to me having the strongest voice, even if it was far from the finished article! Finding time to make the band a priority was one of the hardest things during the late 90s. Being three years younger than the others meant that I was off on a gap year and then to university while they were finishing up their degrees in London. Nevertheless, we did manage to keep meeting up, playing and recording during this time. When I returned from six months in South Africa in 1998, I was greeted by Richard at the airport with the news that our first gig was ten days away. The infamous Hope & Anchor show is something of a benchmark in my memory. The terror and exhilaration of playing live, the acid test that is putting yourselves and your songs out into the world and this glimpse into the London band scene were very motivating and seductive feelings. Much to everyone's surprise, I had been able to learn all the lyrics for the songs, but I also realised that there's a lot more to being a frontman than just getting that bit right…

The following year continued the stuttering theme as I embarked on my first year at Edinburgh University. While I was having a lot of debauched fun, thoughts of London and the band were never far from my mind. In the summer of 1999, after a lengthy chat with Tim, I decided to defer my degree and move to London to try and make it with Keane.

I've got real ambivalence about our time living in London. On the surface, in the course of two years, it looks as though we didn't really achieve anything. But the truth is that it was a time when we learned a huge amount about ourselves and our abilities. Oftentimes it was a grind – commuting into central London on the 73 bus and working day jobs lugging boxes and putting numbers in computers. But in the evenings, we would devote ourselves to the music. Tim, Dominic and I shared a flat in Stoke Newington where we would write and record and there were twice-weekly visits to the amusingly dank Backstreet rehearsal rooms on Holloway Road. Through clouds of dope smoke (mostly created by me) songs, both good and bad, were written, rehearsed and recorded. There were also monthly gigs in Camden that focused our minds and forced us to improve as performers, even if it was just our long-suffering friends and family in the audience. In fact, a few years ago footage surfaced of a show we did at the Bull & Gate – we look a bit wooden, but you can see *something* emerging. As a singer I think my voice had definitely improved (less flat, gradually conveying more emotion) and I'd begun to understand the importance of communicating with a crowd. However, I remember doing shows with Coldplay during that time and thinking Chris had this amazing charisma that seemed so infectious. Despite my best efforts I knew I was still a long way from that.

Even if our two years in London featured more downs than ups, the dynamics of the band really began to emerge, particularly Tim's songwriting and my singing. The gigs taught us that we needed to have succinct, memorable and meaningful songs and that I really needed to sell them in a believable way as a frontman. My voice definitely matured during this time – it became much more of an expression of me, as opposed to a pastiche of my heroes and I think I gradually began to feel less shy and terrified on stage.

In 2001 we left London and took up the offer to live in France for a summer with a producer called James Sanger. My recollection is that James spent brief bits of time recording vocals with me, trying to eke out as much of the 'real me' as he could. Learning to lay down vocals in a studio is a bit of an art form. Unlike live shows where you're trying to connect on a grander scale, recording vocals is more like singing gently into someone's ear. The dynamics are much more pronounced and if you get it right, there's an intimacy that can lift a song into a sublime place. I don't remember really ever achieving this with James, but it was definitely a process that contributed to the way my vocals would end up sounding on *Hopes and Fears*.

If London had felt like stuttering progress, our time in France and the following two years camped at Tim's parents' house back in Sussex became the time when things truly began to fall into place. Dominic had left the band and forced us into our strange setup of piano, drums and voice. That sparse sound, with all the remnants of electronica and programming we had gleaned from working with James would form the basis for what we would become. Tim's writing became more prolific and more potent, and it was my job to help connect those songs with an audience. Most of the time that audience was Tim's mum or dad returning from work to hear our latest efforts, but they were honest in their critiquing, especially Tim's mum, who was never shy of pointing out if I was singing flat.

For whatever reason, something magical happened in that room during those months – the culmination of a lot of hard work and the realisation of a dream. Even if you steadfastly believe in yourselves (like we must have done through the hard times), until you feel that undeniable magic, you don't really know if you have what it takes.

2002 to 2003 was a period of extreme change. We went from the isolation of that room to being chased by every record label in the UK, even heading to America to talk to all the industry bigwigs in New York and LA. The gigging started to ramp up too and all those years of practice began to pay off. It sort of gave the impression that we'd just arrived on the scene fully formed. If only they knew!

I loved the madness of piling into a rented van, me (totally illegally) camped in the back with all the amps, and taking long drives to Middlesborough or Manchester to play shows. The fanbase started to grow and the exhilaration of playing all these great songs live was addictive. There was something very special about the thrill of feeling we were in the ascendancy. A record deal with Island soon followed and that long-awaited wish to make our first album had finally arrived.

I don't remember a huge amount about the recording sessions for *Hopes and Fears*, other than the copious food provided by Heidi at Heliocentric and the sheer joy and excitement of being in a proper studio. Andy Green, our producer, was the perfect man to capture what we had as a band. It was the first time I'd ever been in a vocal booth – basically a little soundproofed cabin with a microphone and a window back out into the studio. It can often feel a bit isolated but Andy (and Tim alongside) were very helpful and encouraging after each take, feeding back their thoughts and notes to me via my headphones.

When I listen back to *Hopes and Fears*, there's a lovely contrast of rawness and purity to the singing – as though I'd only just arrived at the point of being able to sing as well as that. Although I'd had a comfortable upbringing, I had become quite unhappy as a teenager; very closed off, self-conscious and hopeless at managing my emotional world. I think I can hear a person who was able to channel that underlying sadness into those songs that Tim had written.

We used to laugh about an imaginary 'emotion dial' that I would sometimes need to crank up. Even though this might seem a bit contrived, it was really just a way of drawing on that dark place inside me to help imbue the songs with soul and character. Looking back 20 years later, I know it was that dark place that would set me unravelling during the peak of the band's success; but it was also the part of me that had spurred me on and made me the singer that I was.

Tom Chaplin
August 2024

Hastings Beer Festival, June 2005
Photo: Kerry Heary

Don't say Admire
Don't MR!

Naturalness

BEFORE
Started unbelly

Nothing in yr way

On a day like today

The harder you try, the more you back it up

Cntst statement

Flambure Snake

This has no time

SHORT + CLEAR
DON'T RAMBLE.

u know what
likes about
you a.
unorganised me
tickled around
WRECKING
ANSWER
She lunched me
around.

Battle, c. 1998

ALMONRY TRACKS
BEND AND BREAK (A)
EVERYBODY'S CHANGING (A)
YOUR EYES OPEN (A/B)
UNTITLED 1 (A/B)
SOMEWHERE ONLY WE KNOW (A/B)
BING CROSBY NUMBER (A/B)

NEED WORK   (B-SIDES ?)
WONDERFUL RIVER
DO YOU EVER FEEL SICK
INTO THE LIGHT
THE RIGHT WORDS AT THE WRONG TIME
ON A DAY LIKE TODAY

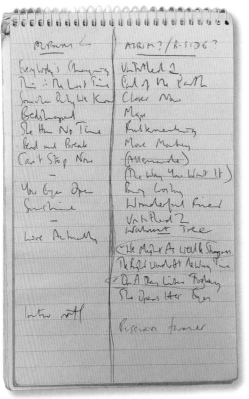
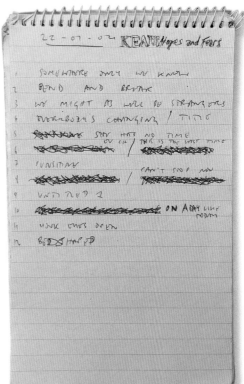

THE OK COMPUTER TEST

1	AIRBAG	SOMEWHERE ONLY WE KNOW
2	PARANOID ANDROID	THIS IS THE LAST TIME
3	SUBTERRANEAN HOMESICK ALIEN	SUNSHINE
4	EXIT MUSIC	WE MIGHT AS WELL BE STRANGERS
5	LET DOWN	BEND AND BREAK
6	KARMA POLICE	EVERYBODY'S CHANGING
7	FITTER HAPPIER	LOVE SONG
8	ELECTIONEERING	CAN'T STOP NOW
9	CLIMBING UP THE WALLS	UNTITLED 1
10	NO SURPRISES	SHE HAS NO TIME
11	LUCKY	ON A DAY LIKE TODAY
12	THE TOURIST	BEDSHAPED

Album титлез ?

BRAIN
STORM

A conversation
A conversation with Keane
Brainstorm
Help Yourself
Speak for Yourself
We need to talk
We **Should** talk
Bedshaped
Bend and Break*
This Is the Last Time
A Simple Thing

KEANE: Bend and Break

ALBUM NAMES

Prelude
Puppeteer
Colossus
A Spoonful of Sugar
Sleeping Beauty
Bedshaped
Under the Stairs
Into the Sky
Well Done You

Exposure
Overexposure
Luminous Beings

Icebreaker

STILLNESS

FOCUS
+

SILENCE

MYSTERY

CHARISMA

SET OF STORIES
FOLK ELEMENT?

MODERN FOLK?
→ AGELESS QUALITIES

Heavenly quality
of love / life
organic +
Distilling darkness of pressing stress
modern discourse
to parts of
love / friendship
SIMPLICITY?
Reinventing
mystery

Stamford Hill, *c.* 2003
Photo: Adam Tudhope

Direct
Uncluttered
Populist
Simple
Vivid

Journeys and conversations

————————

ARTS COVERS

Not too cool
Not too Box office ((humorous?))
Not too arty

Bold + simple
— not over-clever
Say something immediate +
direct, like the music, while
also having enough mystery
and depth to draw people in.

Classic + Bold rather than
"messy indie" note.

[Classic not indie]

BOLD BUT NOT EXPLICIT

[FL]

[LYRICS | RH]

[UNDER | TL]

[UNDER | TRO]

[HANS]

[BC]

NOT PREACHY.

Invite people in to figure out
for themselves, not "Listen
to all our clever opinions,
accept our perspective."

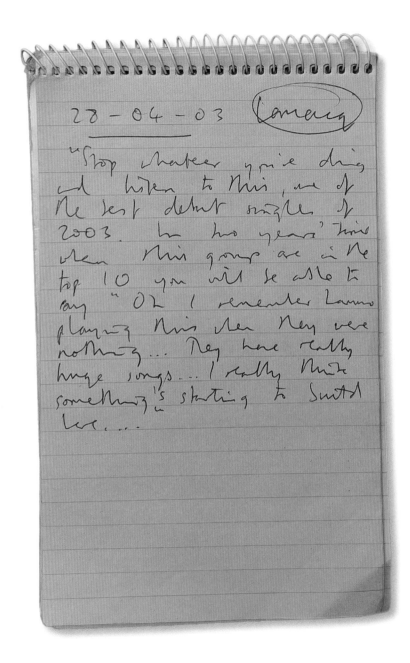

Steve Lamacq quote, transcribed from the first playing
of 'Everybody's Changing' on Radio 1, April 2003

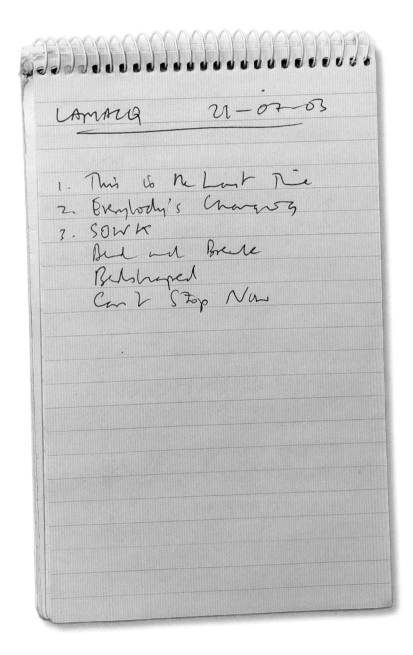

LAMACQ   21 - 07 - 03

1. This is the Last Time
2. Everybody's Changing
3. SOWK
   Bed and Breate
   Bedshaped
   Can't Stop Now

Lamacq Live set list, July 2003

KEANE

Cordially invite you to the launch of their debut album
HOPES AND FEARS

The Highgate Bar
79 Highgate Road NW5
(turn left out of Kentish Town Forum and 500m on left)

Monday 10th May
11pm til late
No admittance without invite

AND IF YOU HAVE A MINUTE
WHY DON'T WE GO
TALK ABOUT IT SOMEWHERE ONLY WE KNOW
THIS COULD BE THE END OF EVERYTHING
SO WHY DON'T WE GO
SOMEWHERE ONLY WE KNOW
(DELAY TO THE END)

THINGS TO DO   05-11-02
_____

1. Get "Somewhere only we know"
   sounding good.

SOMEWHERE ONLY WE KNOW

I walked across an empty land
I knew the pathway like the back of my hand
I felt the earth beneath my feet
Sat by the river and it made me complete

Oh simple thing where have you gone?
I'm getting old and I need something to rely on
So tell me when you're gonna let me in
I'm getting tired and I need somewhere to begin

I came across a fallen tree
I felt the branches of it looking at me
Is this the place we used to love?
Is this the place that I've been dreaming of?

Oh simple thing where have you gone?
I'm getting old and I need something to rely on
So tell me when you're gonna let me in
I'm getting tired and I need somewhere to begin

And if you have a minute why don't we go
Talk about it somewhere only we know?
This could be the end of everything
So why don't we go somewhere only we know?

SOMEWHERE ONLY WE KNOW

1. Sort out drums
2. New vocal
3. New piano
4. Bass
5. Big part in chorus
6. BVs?
7. Part for M8 — ARP?
8. Sort out mill at end.

Recording notes, Tim's notebooks

An interesting thing about 'Somewhere Only We Know' is that it really includes so many of the themes of the album in one song. Maybe that's why it became such a defining track for us. The bond with our hometown, how intertwined we were with the natural world, the anxiety about time slipping away, most importantly the belief in friendship and persevering together – it's all contained within the relatively concise lyrics. As the years went by and we struggled to get our music heard, it felt more and more like we were looking for answers – from each other, from the trees even! We would often go out for a drink in Battle and to walk back to my parents' house meant navigating a completely unlit footpath through the backstreets and across the fields, so on a dark night you literally had to feel your way in total blackness, trying not to fall down the steep steps to Manser's Shaw. The chorus lyrics were repurposed from an earlier unfinished song from maybe 1999 or 2000 – it was a bit of a dirge, and the only decent bit of the song was the lyrics "so why don't we go somewhere only we know". It had a slightly mysterious, magical ring to it, and it was pleasing that it found its place eventually.

TR-O

After two years in London and a beautiful but strange summer in France, in 2002 we returned to our parents' houses to try and give ourselves the best chance of focussing on our music without interruption. With slightly begrudging acceptance (or did we just move in?), Tim's Mum and Dad let us take over a room at their house. They'd often return from work and be the guinea pigs for new songs or arrangements, mostly nodding in proud approval, as the faint smell of an overloaded fuse box wafted through the house. It was in this room that I can vividly recall Richard and I listening to Tim's first demo of 'Somewhere Only We Know'. What I remember most is that the "simple thing" section came in and I just assumed that it was the chorus, so there was a real feeling of surprise and elation as the actual chorus "if you have minute" rose up. I don't think we were in any doubt that it was great song - did we know we had a song that would change our lives and become such an anthem? I doubt it!

Of all the billions of times that song has been listened to, I feel such a sense of honour that I was the first. People ask if I ever get bored of singing it – the answer is always "no" – it holds such an important place in people's hearts that it never fails to lift me up like it did that very first time.

TC

'Somewhere Only We Know' video shoot, Chiddingly, January 2001
Photo: Alex Lake

BOND & BREAK

When you when you forget your name
When blank faces all look the same

Meet me in the morning when you wake up
Meet me ~~After you're someone else~~
in the morning, then you'll wake up
~~love your eyes, release yourself~~

World-sick, bitter and hardened heart
Aching, waiting for night
Waiting for life to start

Meet me in the morning the you'll wake up

~~If only I don't~~
Without you I will seal and break
I'll meet you on the other side
I'll meet you in the light
~~Without you~~ I will suffocate
I'll meet you in the morning when you wake.

BEND AND BREAK

When you, when you forget your name
When old faces all look the same
Meet me in the morning when you wake up
Meet me in the morning then you'll wake up

If only I don't bend and break
I'll meet you on the other side
I'll meet you in the light
If only I don't suffocate
I'll meet you in the morning when you wake

Bitter and hardened heart
Aching, waiting for life to start
Meet me in the morning when you wake up
Meet me in the morning then you'll wake up

If only I don't bend and break
I'll meet you on the other side
I'll meet you in the light
If only I don't suffocate
I'll meet you in the morning when you wake

Bend or break

Intro   -   just hats + bd   • • •• • •• • •• ••
V1   -   "   + "
Br 1   -   "   +   "
~~Ch1~~ V2-   •• •• • •• •|• •• •• ••
                   • • • •|•
Br 2   fill in at ½ + end   has cowbell 1234 (feet?)
Chorus 1   has tamb w snare + cowbell
Instr   lose cowb/tamb   - quiet hat
V3   ••   ••   ••
Br 3   as br 2
Ch2   as   Ch1
Break 1   hats only 4 bars
          then normal drums 8 bars
Break 2   ~~bread~~ hats only
          Ch 3   as   prev Chorus
DrumsEnds   at end of Ch Piano/Strings outro.

In a way this is the essential song of the album for me. You can feel the straining to keep going in the face of seemingly endless knock-backs; the promise to support each other and the desperate need for each other's strength and encouragement. We used to meet almost every day to work on music or talk about music. At some point, probably multiple points, we each had a crisis of faith – and we badly needed each other's passion and conviction to believe that what we were doing was worth something.

TR-O

Hopes and Fears was really the culmination of many long years of mistakes, hard work and bloody-mindedness! I think we felt this very acutely during 2002. We sensed that most of our friends and families thought we were mad to still be pursuing our dreams. The plan of making it via the Camden scene had failed and, despite our best efforts, we had to endure seemingly endless indifference from record labels. I'm glad that we had enough resolve to double down and keep working at it. A set of friendships forged in childhood are at the core of Keane and I feel like 'Bend and Break' sums this up. Let's meet up, let's lean on each other, let's get through to the other side.

TC

I would really like
to meet you in daylight

Strangers DVD cover art
Photo: Alex Lake

WE MIGHT AS WELL BE STRANGERS

I don't know your face no more
Or feel the touch that I adore
I don't know your face no more
It's just a place I'm looking for

We might as well be strangers in another town
We might as well be living in a different world
We might as well

I don't know your thoughts these days
We're strangers in an empty space
I don't understand your heart
It's easier to be apart

We might as well be strangers in another town
We might as well be living in another time
We might as well be strangers

For all I know of you now
For all I know

Strangers

Vocals generally pretty good.
bars 2 + 4 in V1 re-do.
+ C1 ?

bars 1,2 + 4 in V2 re-do.

C2 OK? except first
"it might as well."

Big section here deeper?

Fade things quicker / quieter?

Otherwise brilliant.

My recollection is that Richard was going through a nasty break-up, and this song came out of that. He was the first of us to live with a girlfriend, and I think there's something more traumatic about breaking up when you've shared that way of life with someone. It was the first time we'd encountered the concept of going from sharing a life quite intensively to becoming like strangers again.

TR-O

'Strangers' was a real latecomer and we had to learn it very quickly in the studio. I think the song articulates the nature of a failed relationship so beautifully – how we can go from a place of feeling such deep connection to a place of total estrangement. It's interesting to me that this song continues to create such a moment in our live shows all these years later – I suppose that's partly the drama of the ending but also the fact that broken heartedness will forever be a rite of passage!

TC

WE MIGHT AS WELL BE STRANGERS

I don't know you feel no more adore
There's nothing ...
I don't know your feel no more
It's just a place I'm looking for

We might as well be strangers in another town
we might as well be living in a different world
we might as well . . . .   (x3)

I don't know your thoughts these days
& you're living in a different place
I don't understand your heart
it's easier to be apart
(Chorus)

We might as well be strangers in another town
we might as well be living in another time
we might as well, we might as well,
we might as well be strangers
for all I know if you now (x3)
for all I know.

I feel like an idiot
and I'm losing time
at a steady pace
I've been trying to change
but things never change
you never get any better
you never get it out of
your system

[we might aswell be strangers]

We can see through each other.

EVERYBODY'S CHANGING

You say you wander your own land
But when I think about it I don't see how you can
You're aching, you're breaking
And I can see the pain in your eyes
Says everybody's changing
And I don't know why

So little time
Try to understand that I'm
Trying to make a move just to stay in the game
I try to stay awake and remember my name
But everybody's changing
And I don't feel the same

You're gone from here
Soon you will disappear
Fading into beautiful light
Because everybody's changing
And I don't feel right

OV CH notes   18/1/52

Intro (Piano with louder?)
        live piano louder?

V1   ✓

V2   ✓
Break   — live piano up a bit?
C1   I'm quiet
          (can't quiet) ~~up louder~~
    esp "everybody's crossing..." ~~up and~~
           clav louder?
_____
Break ✓
V3   ✓
C2   ~~clav louder from~~ vocal lead
        "I'm" quiet   seems better
M8   Piano mix out more?
          clav fills at end louder
C3   Strings great Crash louder
      More OT?   on first beat?

Vocal seems quieter for
last few bars esp "I'm"
"try-g to stay awake → ed"
clav fills at ~3.19 a bit louder

One effect of time passing – we moved to London for a while, met lots of new people, were getting older and grappling with the frustrations of what we wanted to do with our music – was that it put a strain on our friendships. The three of us had a really intense friendship and were already spending huge amounts of time together (and we hadn't even started touring properly yet!) – and sooner or later that had to change. We all wanted to find our own individual identities, to carve out our own space. To me this song is about the bittersweetness of watching that brotherly friendship change into something else – something more sustainable and equally beautiful, but also less intoxicating.

TR-O

The first thing that always springs to mind when I think of 'Everybody's Changing' is hearing it for the first time on Radio 1. We had heard that Steve Lamacq had come to a gig and wanted to play the song on his evening show. We gathered round the radio at home and even cracked out a bottle of champagne – regardless of what would happen next, it felt like such a breakthrough that it warranted some real celebration. Just to know that someone we really respected was on our side and hearing it over the airwaves was a genuinely lovely, triumphant moment. Interestingly the lyrics are so much about the struggle of feeling we were being left behind and so the irony of it being the song that got us our break is not lost on me!

TC

Everybody's Changing

Intro cool .
V1   cool
V2   ok   + join

C1 good . Strings in . Vox DT Rvs?
            Channel louder ?
              Toms louder
Join after C1 a bit weak
Em bit good .
V3   good . timing ?
Join after V3 need a bit more?
C2   an   C 1

M8 needs to be step-up from C2.
      More like intro ?
         Strings

C3 bigger . New strings .
          Low STR2 / Hi 'Solea?
Beef up snare ? in choruses.

XFM Session, 2005
Photo: Kerry Heary

Everybody's Changing

Intro 1 -   Tim   4 bars
      2 -   Drums (no snare, just pad / bd / hat)
V1 -   pad / bd / hat
V2 - Snare + pad / bd / hat
Ch 1 - Ride + Sn + bd + hat + pad
V3 - (as V2)   snare + pad / bd / hat
Ch 2 - Ride + Sn - bd + hat + pad
A minor section 2 bars   - bd   only
Middle (Solo) - as Choruses   ~~Snare half speed~~ bd / hat / Ride
A minor section   - bd only
Chorus 3
End

NEO

Dodgy drum fills

Needs tambourine
and/or
something else 16th-y.

Solo a bit demo-y moog? Arp?

Something 4-to-the-floor-y
on snare?

Something to keep up drums.

High strong line
Doubler in 1st bar
intro + ptn
verse
Clean pattern in V1

OH in chorus ...?

Feedback ...

YOUR EYES OPEN

Well it's a lonely road that you have chosen
Morning comes
And you don't want to know me anymore
And it's a long time since your heart was frozen
Morning comes
And you don't want to know me anymore

For a moment your eyes open and you know
All the things I ever wanted you to know
I don't know you and I don't want to
Till the moment your eyes open and you know

That it's a lonely place that you have run to
Morning comes
And you don't want to know me anymore
And it's a lonely end that you will come to
Morning comes
And you don't want to know me anymore

Your Eyes Open   snare has
                                                            1 echo

            2 bars then   1234   / 2,4
Intro ⟶ pumping bd + snare , hats — ER1 style   2 x lifts at end of bar.
V1   no Snare 1st half then in
Ch1   as loud verse,   (tamb x16s)
V2   as Ch1
Ch2   as ''   (tamb x 16s)
Instr ＃8 hats + bd only
      ＃8 hat — bd + Sn

Ch 3
~~Outro~~ jam ＃16 2 bars / just drums
      then   Fade outro.

A bit like 'Can't Stop Now', I think there's a lot of fantasy here – trying to convince yourself that you didn't want to be with someone anyway! It reads as a little immature and somewhat spiteful I think… but maybe sometimes that's just what we need to tell yourself in order to get through.

TR-O

By 2002, technology had improved and become cheap enough that a home recording set-up was something we really coveted. A lovely guy called Paul Harris, who had started up his own music publishing firm, was one of a handful of people who really believed in us and he found us the money to buy an Apple computer. Finally, we were able to start making some half-decent home recordings. We did this a lot in tandem with rehearsing, fine-tuning the songs. 'Your Eyes Open' is definitely an example of this – lots of nice production ideas that percolated over time.

It also turned out to be the solution to the conundrum of having lost a member of the band. Suddenly we could run bass or keyboard tracks off the computer, which allowed Tim to focus on playing the piano.

TC

Wireless Festival, 2005
Photo: Kerry Heary

SHE HAS NO TIME

You think your days are uneventful
And no one ever thinks about you
She goes her own way
She goes her own way

You think your days are ordinary
And no one ever thinks about you
But we're all the same
And she can hardly breathe without you

She says she has no time for you now
She says she has no time

Well think about the lonely people
Or think about the day she found you
Or lie to yourself
And see it all dissolve around you

She says she has no time for you now
She says she has no time

Lonely people tumble downwards
And my heart opens up to you
When she says she has no time for you now
She says she has no time

Dm   G   C/E   Fmaj7

Dm   Am G Dm   Am   G

Dm   G   C/G   Fmaj7

Dm   Am G   Dm   G

C   G   Am   G   Fmaj7
D
C   G   Am   G   Fmaj7

'She Has No Time' chord progression

This was the earliest song that made it onto the album, and we recorded quite a few versions of it over the years. It was definitely influenced by Sigur Rós and was an attempt at emulating their floaty, ethereal melodies that seemed so simple but were so powerful. Tom and I were living together in a very dingy flat in Stamford Hill and I remember him coming home one night very agitated because he was evidently being strung along by a girl he was crazy about. It wasn't his usual style to get so openly upset, so it really struck me – and it turned into this song. Writing-wise, it was perhaps the first time we felt we'd written something concise but powerful – it felt kind of perfectly formed, like it was exactly what it was supposed to be.

TR-O

'She Has No Time' is such a memorable and important song for me. Tim wrote it when we were living in London as a message of solidarity in heartbreak after I had been repeatedly knocked back by a girl I really fancied. It was really the first time that we felt we had a song that seemed to resonate on a deeper emotional level. It went through many recorded versions while we were still a guitar band, recording on an ADAT machine that we'd borrowed. I remember a particularly beautiful guitar solo. I suppose it also coincided with me really finding my voice as a singer – no longer trying to mimic my idols but channelling my own experience and soulfulness into something more uniquely me. The song was personal with a soaring melody, all things that allowed me to unlock this part of myself.

TC

She Has No Time   *[crossed out]*

laid back
Kit w.
teardrop bd

Intro 4 bars → Teardrop bass   again TITLT + rev snare   808 again + Reverb ?/Delay

NOTHING — V1   first half just bd
~~[crossed out]~~ Hat + sn + bd 2nd " hi hat +

Hat   Ch1 has 2nd snare patt + harder hats - keep as ⌐ , raised hats

Hat   V3 as above - drums all through

Ride   Ch2 into Instr "hat solo!

Hat   Instr as above

Ride ⌐ "Lonely people" - more driving hats   but keep as above
     ⌐ Ch 3

Ride. Outro - drums ~~back~~ keep on   with rev-snare
          2̶4̶ 1̶6̶ bars ?
              16

TRY HOT RODS   V hat
                          Ch Ride
                          Instr - Hat

                    Ting on   Ride at end

SUN HAS NO TIME
_____

Intro great. Make last note sustain?
V1 - make JC's Dream pad
    a little less space-y?
V2 - duck JC's Dream pad
    down ... bit in-your-face &
    present.
C1 - lovely.

V3 - same synth pad.
C2 - try shaker / tams?

Solo - ARP is slightly earlier?

M8 - Sing some huskier string i ??
        Does sound nice.
C3 - open up into lush C3.
Outro - cf demo. (Riff still clicky)
Generally lovely.

Berlin, 2004
Photo: Alex Lake

CAN'T STOP NOW

I noticed tonight
That the world has been turning
While I've been stood here dithering around
Though I know I said I'd wait around till you need me,
I have to go
I hate to let you down

But I can't stop now
I've got troubles of my own
Because I'm short on time
I'm lonely and I'm too tired to talk

I noticed tonight
That the world has been turning
While I've been stuck here withering away
Though I know I said I wouldn't leave you behind
But I have to go
It breaks my heart to say

That I can't stop now
I've got troubles of my own
Because I'm short on time
I'm lonely and I'm too tired to talk
To no one back home
I've got troubles of my own
And I can't slow down for no one in town
And I can't stop now for no one

And I can't slow down for no one in town
And I can't stop now for no one

The motion keeps my heart running

I've been stood here
dithering around
Though I know I said I'd wait
around till you need me

Though I know I said
I'd never wouldn't leave
you behind

Tom Chaplin
x

Tom Chaplin
x

My inability to get over break-ups started early… and this one had taken me years. By this point in the process I was really trying to push myself forward, and our music and our desire to be heard gave me a focus. There's a big element of fantasy in this song – an imaginary scenario in which I might say to this person who I was so haunted by, 'Sorry, but I don't have time for this anymore.' In that respect, it's really a 'message to self' to move on. And I think the reprise section of the song is a recognition that sometimes we just try to keep busy in order to avoid facing the emotions we don't want to face.

TR-O

Whilst I can't recall how 'Can't Stop Now' came together, it's a great song which really sums up how we all felt at the time; rushing around but seemingly going nowhere…

TC

CSN

F   Am   Bb   F   (last time:)
                                    g

Bb/D   Csus4   F   Bb

Gm   Bb/c
_____

Dm   Bb   Bb   F

Dm   Am   (Bb   F)
                          x2
                    → Bb   Bb/c

_____

Dm   Eb6   Bb   C

D   F#m7

I can't stop now
I've got troubles [Emaj7] my own [59/C#]
coz I'm short [Em] home [A]
I'm lonely [D7/F#] and I [G] too hard
to [F#m] to no one [Em7]

I can't stop now → back home
I've got troubles of my own
and I can't stop now slow down
for no one in town
no I can't stop now
for no one.

Sunshine   Sound - Funky

Washy cymbals? {
Intro - no drums
V1 - " "
Br1 (but if I'm one thing...) - no drums
Ch1 - no drums

Hats | Instr - Drums   .. ..   get middle one louder
Hats | V2   "
Hats | Br2   "   break at end of Br2
Ride | Ch2   "
Hats | Instr - ½ "   [break at end on 1]
Ride | Ch3   "
Ride~~Hats~~ | Instr - occasional breaks.

                                          breaks on
End is 2 sung Choruses   3.
        1 instrumental (4× tom riffs)

Vol of TD-7 is 1 mark left of middle.

SUNSHINE

I hold you in my hands
A little animal
And only some dumb idiot would let you go
But if I'm one thing then that's the one thing
I should know

Can anybody find their home?
Out of everyone can anybody find their home?

I hold you in cupped hands
And shield you from a storm
Where only some dumb idiot would let you go
But if I'm one thing then that's the one thing
I should know

Can anybody find their home?
Out of everyone can anybody find their home?
Lost in the sun can anybody find their home?
Come on, come on, come on
Can anybody find their home?

Bag of
extenuating
circumstances.

Blue Moon
Moon River

In 2001 we spent several months in France recording what was supposed to be our album. We did a lot of good work out there but didn't write many new songs. But one sunny evening I took myself off away from everyone else and sat in a field trying to be Nick Drake. It's one of the few 'happy' songs I've ever written, but even then the lyrics are cut through with an anxious sense of not trusting yourself with someone else's heart – the feeling that you'll always be searching.

TR-O

One of the most eventful chapters of the Keane story pre *Hopes and Fears* was the time we spent in France with James Sanger in the summer of 2001. We met James via Mark Wallis, who'd helped to produce some early demos and gave us a shot in a real studio. James had real charisma and an enthusiasm to help us develop our sound, so he invited us out to his dilapidated farm house in Normandy. The experience was really crucial in so many ways, even if it did end in tears!

Dominic, our guitarist, had left the band, so we had to find a new way of presenting the music. Tim had also hit a roll with his writing, so we wanted to make the most of these new songs. James taught us about production and programming and gave us the confidence to see beyond Dominic's departure. Gradually a blend of piano and electronica began to emerge as the backbone to our sound. The combination of my voice, this new sound and some great songs meant that we were beginning to feel like we had something unique. During those long summer days, Tim could often be found under the shade of trees, guitar in hand, writing away. I can only assume that's where this song started its life. With the end of summer came the end of the dream with James – lovely as he was, his behaviour became erratic and we took this as our cue to return home.

TC

[Em]   [Eb+/E]
I hold you in my hands
[Em7]   [Eb+/E]
a little animal
[Em]   [B+E]   [Em7]
and after some dumb idiot would let you go
    [Am]
but if I'm one too
               [D]
                                        [Bbmaj7]
                          [B]
Now that's one thing
          [D]   [Dmaj7]
I should know
              [Bm]   [D9+5]
can anybody find their home

out of everyone can anybody find their ho

look in the same can anybody . . .

come on come on come on

A#   D   E   F#

A#maj   A#   D#   F   D#
A#mi   A#   C#   F

F = 698.60/13

659.26   ±13

F# higher 695

C F Bb   739.98   1479.

                              x2

[scribbled out text]

You tell me
~~[scribbled]~~ Of a land
a dry and dusty world
where only some dumb ???
would dare to go

I hold you in my heads
in my ??? world
I can't ??? anything
without you ???

'This Is The Last Time' video shoot contact sheet

Photos: Mark Guthrie

This is the last time   No double hats?

FILLS INTO CHORUS

Intro - bd / rim shot   to cut cymbal -

V1 - no drums 1st half

RIM SHOT   - "sweep it into the corner"   ~~double hi hat~~ ~~to trashy~~ early   single hat
CRASH   snare   1 2 3 4
RIM SHOT   B1   double hat w quite 808 bd   w. rim shot

SN   Ch   more open bd part, same snare (regular)

RS   break - hats ~~then~~ ~~early snare bd for~~ 2nd half of break   as intro

CRASH   RS   V2 - ~~hats / bd / early snare~~   ~~single~~ hat / rim shot   1234
Check in mix RS B2 - " " ~~regular~~ snare , do as above

SN   Ch2   same as   B1   rim shot
Instr 1 as B1   with fills   Verse2
Ch3 as Ch - reg snare
Instr 2 as inst 1.   bd

                     ✳ building crash into Bridge
                     ✳ Bridge - Fast Ride w rim shot
                      Funkier double bd in 2nd ½ of V2

HOT RODS
               real bass

Intro - Teardrop / rim shot
loud break - no drums
V1 - no drums 1st ½ then real bd / rim shot   build crash into B1
B1 - as ~~✳~~ V1 ride longer fill into Ch1
Ch1 - snare / ride / bd   hat
break - as intro (teardrop)   Instr as ch2 w. fills
V2 - just bd / ~~not~~ rim   crash into B2   2nd ½ hat   Ch3 -   Instr ~~crash~~ Ride
B2 - with ride / rim shot / bd
Ch2 - as Ch1   Roll at end

THIS IS THE LAST TIME

This is the last time
That I will say these words
I remember the first time
The first of many lies
Sweep it into the corner
Or hide it under the bed
Say these things they go away
But they never do

Something I wasn't sure of
But I was in the middle of
Something I forget now
But I've seen too little of

The last time
You fall on me for anything you like
Your one last line
You fall on me for anything you like
And years make everything alright
You fall on me for anything you like
And I, no I don't mind

This is the last time
That I will show my face
One last tender lie
And then I'm out of this place
Tread it into the carpet
Or hide it under the stairs
You say that some things never die
Well I tried and I tried

TILT 1st MIX NOTES

19-07-03

1. Kick needs to punch
through more.

2. Snare drum?
Check snare sound.

3. Less delay on vocal —
save for choruses.

(4) Make riddim sound fuller +
more real.

5. Try "sexy slap" in
choruses?

I remember Tom and I were working in an office in Covent Garden and I had to sneak off to the toilets with my dictaphone to make a note of the bridge section – it randomly popped into my head while I was doing the photocopying. You can really hear the influence of The Smiths in the feel of the track, and also in the slightly melodramatic, slightly barbed, tone of the lyrics. I was proud of 'tread it into the carpet or hide it under the stairs' – that juxtaposition of mundane everyday images with more sweeping emotional statements felt very right for us and it became a distinctive part of our music. I was never totally sure what the message of the song was – it seemed to have slightly conflicting messages, but we decided to embrace that and it seemed to add to the spirit of 'things are a mess right now but time will make sense of it'. It ended up feeling strangely cathartic.

TR-O

I feel like this is a song that really demonstrates why we're more than the sum of our parts as a band. The original demo was a dreamy piano ballad which appeared around the same time as 'She Has No Time'. We'd been listening to a lot of The Smiths and the Morrissey solo albums, *Southpaw Grammar* and *Vauxhall & I* – you could hear a lot of that influence in the original version. The song went on a journey in the years that followed, becoming something much more strident and uplifting once it had my vocals and Richard's drumming.

TC

THIS IS THE LAST TIME

VERSE

^GThis is the last time^D
that I will ^Csay these words^G
I remember the first time^D
the first ^Cof many lies^G
sweep it into the corner
or hide it under the bed
say these things will go away
but they never do

BRIDGE

something I wasn't sure of^{Cmaj7} ^{Bm}
but I was ^{Em}in the middle of^A
something ^{Cmaj7} I forget now^{Bm}
but I've ^{Em}seen to little of

CHORUS

^GThe last time you ^{Bm}call on me ^{Am}
for anything ^Dyou like
your one last time you call on me
for anything you like

and years make everything alright
so fall on me for anything you like
no I don't mind

Em Bm   Am   D

———

this is the last time
that I will show my face
one last tender lie and
~~and~~ then I'm out of this place
tread it into the carpet
or hide it under the stairs
say that some things never die
well I tried and I tried

———

BRIDGE
—
CHORUS

ON A DAY LIKE TODAY

On a day like today
I looked at you and I
saw something in the way
you stared into the sky

I saw you were sick and tired of
my wrong turns

if you only knew
the way I feel
I'd really love to tell you but I

could never seem to say
the words I needed to.
On a day like today
no other words would do.

I saw you were sick and tired of my wrong turns
if you only knew the way I feel
I'd really love to tell you but I
can never find the words to say
and I don't know why.

ON A DAY LIKE TODAY

On a day like today
I looked at you and I
Saw something in the way
You stared into the sky

I saw you were sick and tired
Of my wrong turns
If you only knew the way I feel
I'd really love to tell you

But I could never seem to say
The things I needed to
On a day like today
No other words would do

I saw you were sick and tired
Of my wrong turns
If you only knew the way I feel
I'd really love to tell you
But I can never find the words to say
And I don't know why

I can't find the words to say
And I don't know why

I'm not sure where this song came from. The 'something in the way' is very obviously borrowed from Nirvana. This one felt like a very throwaway thing at first, but the mantra-like repetitiveness and the feeling of never being able to say the right thing, or trying to say the right thing and just making matters worse, definitely has a resonance… most of us experience that feeling at some point or other! We were trying to capture that sickening moment when you know something's over but you're still trying to salvage it.

TR-O

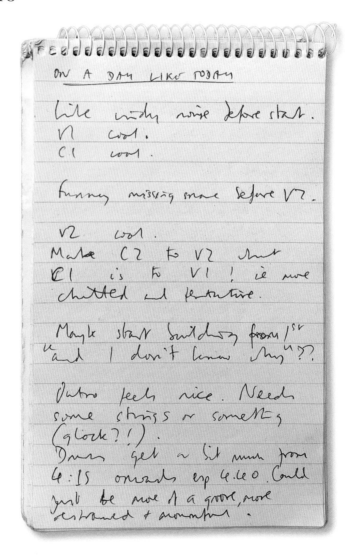

VERSE 1
A house on fire, a wall of stone
a door that once was open
an empty house and empty homes
Who ate your heart?
You're cold inside

CHORUS 1
You're not the one I longed for
I'll see you on the other side (x2)

CHORUS 2
The sad world couldn't show me love
to lie in your heart of hearts
will I ever see you again
and lie in your heart of hearts?

3 CHORUS
Who ate your heart?
You're cold inside
You're not the one I loved for
I'll see you on the other side x2

(CHORUS)

UNTITLED 1

A house on fire
A wall of stone
A door that once was open
An empty face and empty bones

Who ate your heart?
You're cold inside
You're not the one I hoped for
I'll see you on the other side
I'll see you on the other side

The wind wouldn't blow me home
To lie in your heart of hearts
Will I ever see you again
And lie in your heart of hearts?

A train-of-thought lyric and it has slightly nightmarish qualities. It gives the sense that you're trying to get somewhere but you can't. I think it's one of the few love songs on the album – me trying to deal with a break-up which took me years to move on from!

TR-O

UNTITLED 1

1. Try live drums
2. TC vocal
3. Lyrics
4. Name
5. Tidy up strings in 3rd verse.
6. Work out ending
7. Possible countermelody / duet thing.

Untitled 1   filtered ER 1 vibe

Drums   [drum notation]

From start   Intro (~~2~~ bars + keys)

        Pause 1 bar before V1
        V1   in
        Br1 in
        V2   in
        Ch1 same! (falsetto)
        V3   harder -   has bd 1234   harder sound
        ~~break~~ ~~Br2~~   + into Ch 2

Test sketch for 'Bedshaped' video by Dave Lupton

'Bedshaped'. First draft lyrics

BEDSHAPED

Many's the time I ran with you down
The rainy roads of our old town
Many the lives we lived in each day
And buried altogether

Don't laugh at me
Don't look away
You'll follow me back

With the sun in your eyes
And on your own
Bedshaped and legs of stone
You'll knock on my door and up we'll go
In white light
I don't think so
But what do I know?

I know you think I'm holding you down
And I've fallen by the wayside now
And I don't understand the same things as you
But I do

Don't laugh at me
Don't look away
You'll follow me back

With the sun in your eyes
And on your own
Bedshaped and legs of stone
You'll knock on my door and up we'll go
In white light
I don't think so
But what do I know?
What do I know?
I know

BERNHARDT Shut me

16.10.03 (overnight)

V2 — "things as you" a bit quiet??
delay down a touch?

ett 2 — last post up a bit?
turns up ?

m8 — noises lower
pad down ? STARK
singers up - more lead-y

solo - note delay on first ARP note?
(+ again next time)

Vocal in - entry a bit sudden?

I was staying in my old bed at my mum and dad's house and just before I fell asleep, the verse of this song popped into my head. I wrote them down on the back of an envelope. I was thinking about when we used to walk down North Trade Road into Battle. If you wanted to play tennis at the local rec, you had to pay an old lady called Mrs Rogan and she would give you the keys to the courts. The second verse captures the panicky feeling that we were getting left behind, following a stupid dream that wasn't going to lead anywhere and that we should have given up on years earlier. We didn't belong in London and we didn't belong in Battle anymore. I wanted to believe that one day, near the end, we would be reunited with all the people that had left town, lovers who had broken our hearts, friends we didn't see anymore. My mum was a hospital doctor, and she would talk about people who were stuck in hospital for months or years becoming 'bed-shaped' due to lack of movement. I assumed this was a standard medical term, but I think she actually made it up. I thought it was a great-sounding word and used it to represent old age.

TR-O

For all the self-belief we had as a band, you still need to be able to back it up with something that bears out that resolve. For many years, while we were developing as a band, our friends and families seemed to look on with a healthy dollop of scepticism. There weren't any other bands from our school, we lived in the middle of nowhere, there was no scene – it's easy to understand why they viewed it all with suspicion. Whenever I think of 'Bedshaped' I always think of my dad, a lover (and teacher) of English literature, standing in his kitchen declaring that 'Bedshaped' was 'a beautiful piece of poetry'. If we could convince him then surely we were on to something.

TC

1	2	3	4	5	6	7	8
Bus 60				Bus 50 -1.5		Bus -22	Bus -13.2
0	0	0		0	0	0	0
0 (nvm)	+4 ds	0		-24	-5.3	-15	+3.3

20	21	22	23	24	25	26	27	28	29	30	31
			Bus -14.5			-7.0 Bus	Bus +2.0				
					0	0	0	0	0	-33	+3
+27	0	0	0	0							
-25	-76	-33	-25	-33	-33	-32	-6.0	0	-3.8	-10	-

IX LEVELS

10	11	12	13	14	15	16	17	18	19
	Bus +1.8			Bus 8.0					
			+28	0					
0	○	0		0	0	0	0	0	0
-26	-26	-32	-32	-20	-18	-17	-19	-14	-16

33	34	35	36	37	38	39	40	41	42	46
				○	0	○	○	0	0	+63
0.0	-14	-16		0	-33	-12	0	0	0	0

Brixton Academy, November 2004
Photo: Alex Lake

THE FIRST TIME I HEARD KEANE

The first time I heard Keane I was working at a music equipment hire company in London called Matt Snowballs. I was based in the warehouse, testing equipment to go out on hire and checking equipment in when it returned. We always had the radio on in the warehouse because everyone who worked there had very narrow taste in music and the radio just about kept us from arguing over what we listened to. Gary and Jef only liked punk, Steve only liked EDM, Kent only liked metal. It was 2004 and British music at the time was dominated by angular-sounding guitar bands. If you wanted to be cool and successful, you needed guitars. But then one day 'Somewhere Only We Know' came over the airwaves for the first time. No spiky electric guitars. In fact nothing really at all that fitted with what was happening in music at the time. It felt defiant. A band that just didn't seem to care about fitting in. I was instantly on board. Amazingly, everyone in that warehouse agreed. Every time the radio played it the person nearest the stereo would turn it up. Everyone loved it.

Musically, 'Somewhere Only We Know' was strident and full of a kind of undeniable steady but insistent vitality. It announced itself unapologetically. Like so many great songs the lyrics made everyone feel like the song could have been written about them. The words are clear and direct but they also have an artistry and ambiguity that stirs up your imagination. To me it is a song that has a beautiful balance of optimism and also a sense of yearning for something that you think you might have lost forever. *Hopes and Fears*.

One of my favourite things about Tim's songwriting is the way he so often writes about 'us'. Many songwriters seem to get caught up on 'me' or 'you'. I feel like that balance of perspectives gives Keane's songs a deeper sense of empathy and universality. Tim's understated 'Englishness' lends itself so well to writing songs that have a small-town intimacy but also feel like they address the human condition. He can make big ideas feel throwaway – 'When we fall in love we're just falling in love with ourselves'. I'm grateful that I get to help record his songs. In exchange he gets to spend time in my amazing company. It's fair.

Playing shows in front of big audiences takes a little getting used to. The easy mistake is to think of the audience as 'one'. But really you have to view an audience as many individuals. When you think like that and look out at them from the stage you get a much stronger sense of the emotional impact that the music has. I often see people in tears. My belief is that being an individual taking part in a communal experience can give you a sort of safety that allows you to release yourself emotionally in a way that you might not usually do. On stage I often feel tearful as well. I'm sure that this is very common for musicians. The emotional side of concerts can be mysterious and beautiful, regardless of what kind of music it is. But I think the most powerful moments at *our* shows are based on the lyrics. When you hear words and get that 'Hey, that's me' feeling, it's comforting. But *shouting* the way you feel at the top of your lungs is about as cathartic as it gets. When hundreds, or even thousands of people are doing the same thing right along next to you it validates your feelings and oftentimes it somehow frees you from something. So yeah, basically, music is just so fucking cool, isn't it?

Jesse Quin
July 2024

Jesse Quin *c.* 2005

KCRW Radio Session, Los Angeles, 2 June 2004
Photo: Alex Lake

The song that gave the album its name (with a bit of help from 'O Little Town of Bethlehem')! This is a classic example of a really peppy Keane melody matched with a largely melancholy lyric. On the other hand, it does have a sense of forward momentum and of accepting that something is over. The spirit of revelation in 'I open my eyes and it's a lovely day' seems to me to come from David Bowie's *Hunky Dory* album, which we listened to a huge amount at the time. The line about 'I'm glad it's over' is borrowed from T S Eliot's *The Waste Land* and was one I'd been wanting to slip into a song for ages!

TR-O

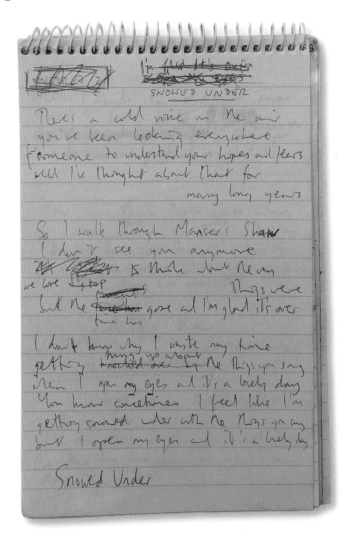

SNOWED UNDER

There's a cold voice on the air
You've been looking everywhere
Someone to understand your hopes and fears
Well, I've thought about that for many long years

So I walk through Manser's Shaw
I don't see you anymore
We love to think about the way things were
But the time has come and I'm glad it's over

I don't know why I waste my time
Getting hung up about the things you say
When I open my eyes and it's a lovely day
You know, sometimes, I feel like I'm
Getting snowed under with the things you say
But I open my eyes and it's a lovely day

Now you think that you're alone
So you make your way back home
I'd love to greet the weary traveller
But your time has gone and I'm glad it's over

I don't know why I waste my time
Getting hung up about the things you say
When I open my eyes and it's a lovely day
You know, sometimes, I feel like I'm
Getting snowed under with the things you say
But I open my eyes and it's a lovely day

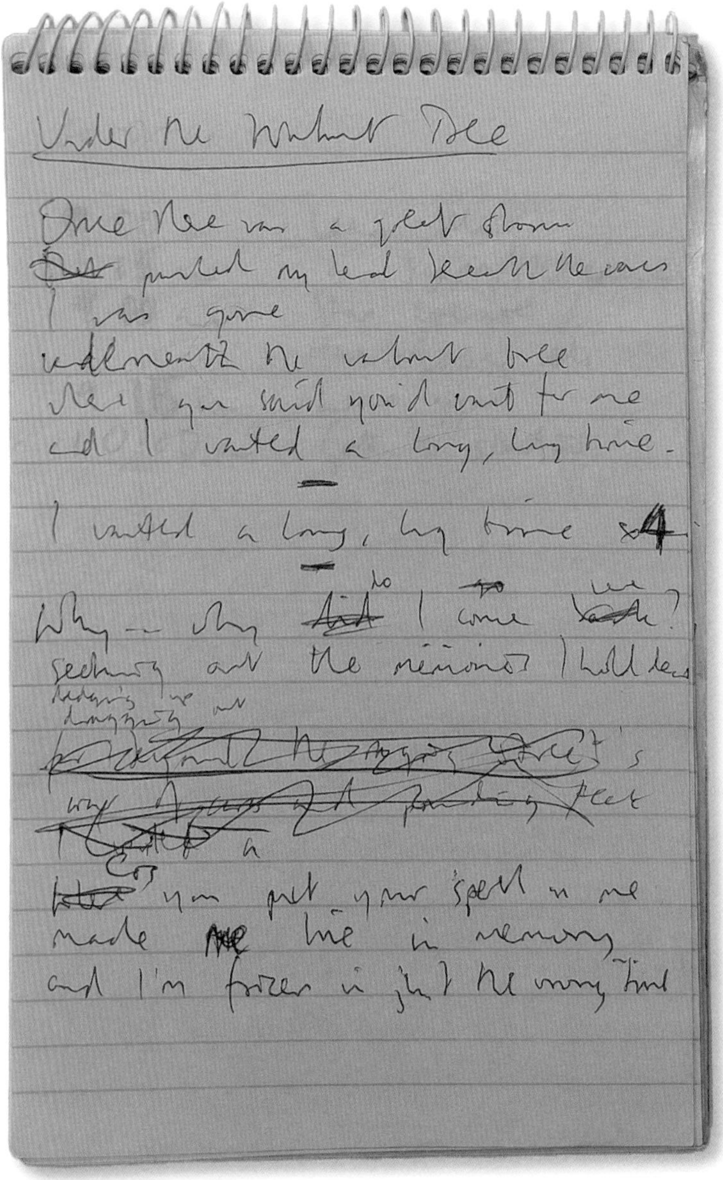

Under the Walnut Tree

Once there was a great storm
~~But~~ pushed my head beneath the caves
I was gone
underneath the walnut tree
Here you said you'd wait for me
and I waited a long, long time.

I waited a long, long time x4

Why -- why ~~did~~ I come ~~back~~ ?
seeking out the memories I still hear

~~[illegible scribbled-out lines]~~

you put your spell on me
made ~~me~~ live in memory
and I'm frozen in just the wrong time

WALNUT TREE

Once there was a great storm
Pushed my head beneath the waves, I was gone

Underneath the walnut tree
Where you said you'd wait for me
And I waited a long, long time

I waited a long, long time
I waited a long, long time
I waited a long, long time
I waited a long, long time

Why, why do I come here?
Seeking out the memories I hold dear

'Cause you put your spell on me
Made me live in memory
And I'm frozen in just the wrong time

I waited a long, long time
I waited a long, long time
I waited a long, long time
I waited a long, long time

The theme of waiting is one that recurs in a lot of our songs at that time! As I've said, I was not good at moving on… James Sanger had a walnut tree in the garden of his place in France – I'd never knowingly seen one before and the image lodged itself in my head and eventually emerged as a song. There's a dreaminess to this song that we revisited (perhaps more effectively) in 'Untitled 1'.

TR-O

WALNUT TREE CHORDS

F# → A♯ min 7 → C♭ min 7 / B♭

C♯ min → C#M sus 4 → B maj 7

F#M → ~ → ~

→ G#A min 7

I remember writing this song quite vividly. I was sat with my Yamaha PSR-48 keyboard on my knees, on a chair in our flat in Stamford Hill. It felt like a major breakthrough, because I sensed that I'd tapped into something that felt energised and flowing melodically but also powerful and authentic lyrically. There's a huge influence from The Smiths on this song and it's a good example of how their flawless marrying of catchy melodies and plaintive lyrics helped us to see how we could bring the best out in our own music. We could write about our somewhat unglamorous lives, lives that felt very rooted in a small town, in a way that could resonate with all sorts of people; and that indulging our love of big melodies didn't have to mean being cheesy or 'too pop'. That balance between peppy melodies and thoughtful lyrics is a hallmark of British songwriting down the years, I think. Lots of imagery that became key to the album – the 'old town', the sense of being trapped, the need to escape – is evident here for the first time.

TR-O

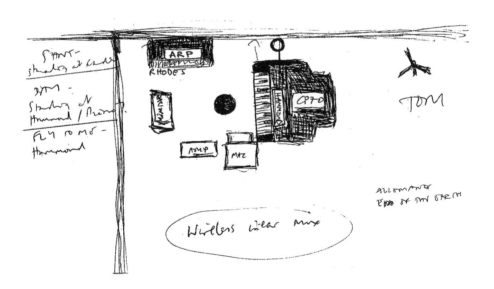

TO THE END OF THE EARTH

Down in the old town
When my mind is wallowing
Round empty hallways
When will I be one again?

You're just making it harder for yourself
Making it easier for everyone else
Making it easier for me

In the old town
You'll never be in and you'll never get out
You learn from the family
You'll never be in and you'll never get out
So run to the end of the earth

Under the archways
When my mind is wallowing
Down to the country
Where I will be well again

You're just making it harder for yourself
Making it easier for everyone else
You're making it easy for me

In the old town
You'll never be in and you'll never get out
You learn from the family
You'll never be in and you'll never get out
So run to the end of the earth

Build me a home underground
Free from light and sound
Build me a home in the air
I will run to the end, to the end
To the end of the earth

By the time we recorded this, we were so busy touring that we had to rush down to the Island Records studios in St Peter's Square for an evening to do the B-sides for whichever single it was. I only had the chorus of this one and can clearly recall sitting on the stairs outside the studio trying to write the rest of the lyrics before Richard finished recording the drums. Steve Winwood's Hammond organ was sitting around in the studio, so we used that for the backbone of the music. Andy Green worked some magic with reverb and echo to create a beautiful dreamscape from what I played. I remember James Sanger used to claim (not without a certain amount of justification) that every big pop song was basically the same as the theme tune to 1970s TV show *Puff the Magic Dragon*. This stuck in my head and I'm certain that's where the line 'live by the sea' crept in from. Given its chaotic origins, it's a deeply emotional song and we were pleased to capture a sense of loss, and of being reunited in some far-distant future, that has echoes of 'Bedshaped'. It's one of my favourite Keane songs.

TR-O

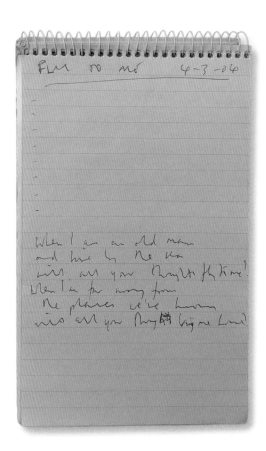

FLY TO ME

Don't turn your back on me, conceal and protect me
I need you to stop me from reeling around
The time's gonna come when you no longer need me
But stay by my side till the sun has gone down

When I am an old man and live by the sea
Will all your thoughts fly to me?

As much as I want you, I can't hold on to you
When will you return to your old home again?
May love lie around you, good fortunes surround you
You know where to turn to when you need a friend

When I am an old man and live by the sea
Will all your thoughts fly to me?
When I am far away from the places we've known
Will all your love bring me home?
Bring me home

This was a very early song compared to the ones that ended up on *Hopes and Fears*. The bouncy swing in the rhythm suggests it was heavily influenced by 60s music, which we were listening to a lot at the time – especially The Kinks. It's interesting that the imagery is located in home, rain, London, waiting for something to happen – themes that we eventually articulated in much more potent ways on the album itself.

TR-O

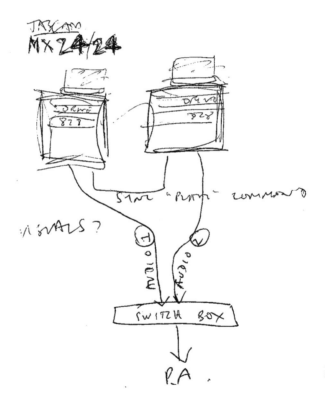

THE WAY YOU WANT IT

From the shelter of your home
As you walk into the rain
Send a message that you know she'll hear
Though she's so far away

Even though you have been wrong before
She'll hear you now
You know she will
But you don't know how

From the shelter of the rain
As you walk into the Tube
As you think of her you wonder
If she thinks about you too

Even though you've waited so long
To see the day
When she will turn to you again
'So long my friend', is what you say

And I don't know why you feel so bad
Where is the life you once had?
And still this horrid feeling
Grows and grows the way you want it to

Even though you've waited so long
To see the day
When she will turn to you again
'So long my friend', is what you say

And I don't know why you feel so bad
Where is the life you once had?
And still this horrid feeling
Grows and grows the way you want it to

You're a fool though, why you feel so bad?
Where is the life you once had?
And still this hollow feeling
Grows and grows the way you want it to

This is quite a rambling, dreamy song compared to a lot of what we were writing at the time. Two things that particularly jump out at me: firstly, the line about changing the world with a song. I sense that's a reflection of the fact that we were beginning to realise how naive we were going into the music industry armed only with good songs and thinking that was enough – we never thought about how we looked or how to make ourselves sound cool or interesting in interviews and so on. In some ways we paid a price for that, in the short term at least. The other notable lyric is the line about an ogre – a bit of fairytale imagery that was starting to creep in to my writing around that time and would be particularly prominent in 'The Frog Prince' (on *Under The Iron Sea*).

TR-O

UNTITLED 2

You chewed me up and you spat me out
The foolish boy that I am
So I chose to wander around and around
And make myself a man

I thought the world could be changed by
A good soul and song
But it's been this way such a long time
So maybe I'm wrong

So long ago it must be
You're still the one that's troubling me
And still so far, so far away
I sat with a tear in my hand on a day so long ago

Inside I am an ogre
With the simple thoughts of a child
I say what I think, and I need to be loved
But I guess that's not your style

So long ago it must be
That you're still the one that's troubling me
And still so far, so far away
I sat with a tear in my hand on a day so long ago

This bears all the marks of having been written in a bit of a hurry! Suddenly we didn't have time to write, so any half-finished ideas we had kicking around were put to work. Again, the theme of waiting crops up.

TR-O

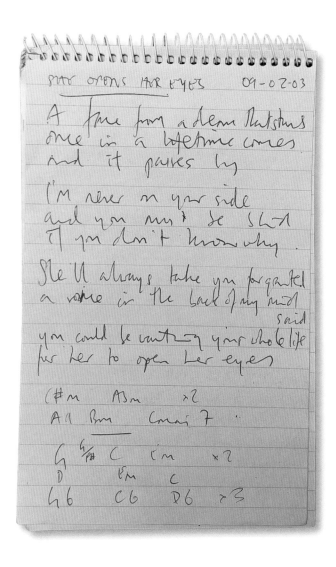

SHE OPENS HER EYES

Your face in a dream returns
Once in a lifetime comes
And it passes by

I'm never on your side
And you must be blind
If you don't know why

She'll always take you for granted
A voice in the back of my mind said
You could be waiting your whole life
For her to open her eyes

I'm never on your side
And you must be blind
If you don't know why

She'll always take you for granted
A voice in the back of my mind said
You could be waiting your whole life
For her to open her eyes
For her to open her eyes

This was a bit of a train of thought, but we all liked its dreamy atmosphere and slightly intangible sense of loss. During the period I wrote it, I was back living with my parents in Battle. A slightly humiliating state of affairs, but they tolerated me playing the piano all day and I started getting better at writing. There was a book of various classical pieces that sat open on the piano for months – my dad would often play from it, but I couldn't read music. One day it was open at a piece called Allemande – by J S Bach, I think – and I just started something based on that word.

TR-O

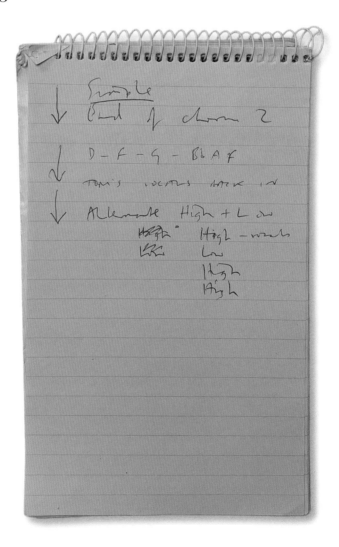

ALLEMANDE

Allemande, where have you gone?
Did I know anything about you?
Many moons have come and gone
They wane so easily without you

All along I said we'd be
Sorry, sorry, and so we are

And ain't that the way that, the way that the wind blows
And ain't that the way that, the way that the wind blows
And ain't that the way that, the way that the wind blows you home
Sorry, sorry, and so we are

Allemande, your face so long
And all my silly hopes hung on you

All along I said we'd be
Sorry, sorry, and so we are

And ain't that the way that, the way that the wind blows
And ain't that the way that, the way that the wind blows
And ain't that the way that, the way that the wind blows you home
Sorry, sorry, and so we are

The way that the wind blows you home
Sorry, sorry, and so we are

Something in me
and my heart

was dying
was heavy as stone

Another rare (for us) happy love song, full of hope and romance and togetherness. That concept of 'Let's take off together and we can live wherever we land', a feeling of freedom to wander, or maybe a restlessness and a need for somewhere or something else, is a theme that has cropped up in our music quite a bit over the years.

TR-O

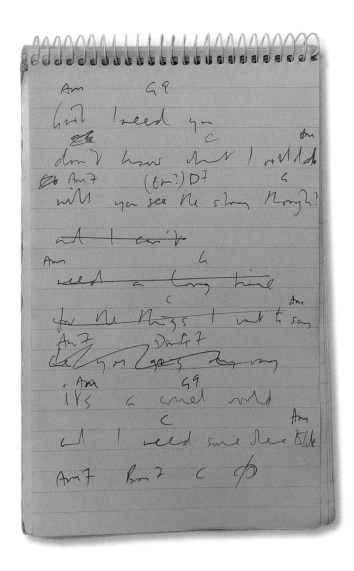

SOMETHING IN ME WAS DYING

Something in me was dying
And my heart was heavy as stone
Hard as I was trying
I never could find, find my way home
And your voice came out of nowhere
"Be my friend and give me your hand
Let's take off together
And then we can live wherever we land"

Something in me was broken
And my thoughts were bitter and ill
My world was blown open
And I couldn't see and I couldn't feel
You said, "Be yourself and think of me
And you'll know there's nothing to fear
Let's make plans together
It's time to move on and get out of here"

Girl, I need you
Don't know what I would do
Will you see the story through?
It's a cruel world
And I need somewhere to hide
But time goes by
And you're still on my side

Something in me was sinking
'Cause my heart was heavy as stone
I gave up, was thinking
I never would find, find my way home
And your voice came out of nowhere
"Be my friend and give me your hand
Let's take off together
And then we can live wherever we land"

Girl, I need you
Don't know what I would do
Will you see the story through?
It's a cruel world
And I need somewhere to hide
The time goes by
And you're still on my side

Waiting, searching
Turning over
Running round in circles
And I've worn myself out
Hoping that we'll always be together
Yeah, we'll always be together

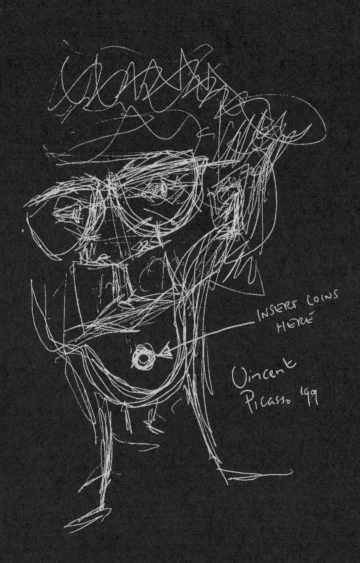

INSERT COINS
HERE

Vincent
Picasso '99

from where I stand

be a candle torn

let's face the truth

it's all love is fear

if I die tomorrow

I'll die a happy man

Brixton Academy, November 2004
Photo: Alex Lake

Cover design by Anna Green at Siulen Design
Book design by Dominic Brookman at Kenosha Design
Illustrations by Tom Chaplin

With thanks to Adam Tudhope, Beth Warren and
Amy MacKenzie at Everybody's Management

© 2024 by Faber Music Ltd & Island Records
(a division of Universal Music Operations Limited)
First published in 2024 by Faber Music and
4wordhouse, on behalf of Island Records
Faber Music
Brownlow Yard
12 Roger Street
London WC1N 2JU

4wordhouse and Island Records are divisions
of Universal Music Operations Limited
4 Pancras Square
London N1C 4AG
fourwordhouse.com
islandrecords.co.uk

All lyrics reproduced by permission of Universal Music
Publishing MGB Ltd. and Hal Leonard Europe Ltd.

ISBN 1 0-571-54328-6
EAN 13: 978-0-571-54328-1

To buy Faber Music publications or to find
out about the full range of titles available
please contact your local retailer or
Faber Music sales enquiries:

Faber Music Limited
Burnt Mill
Elizabeth Way
Harlow
CM20 2HX
England

Tel: +44 (0) 1279 82 89 82
fabermusic.com